The Enduring Legacy

The Enduring Legacy
Essential Family Business Values

Lance Woodbury

Life Stories

Published by Life Stories, Inc.
www.lifestoriesinc.com

Edited by William Long
Cover and Book Design by Jerri Strozier

ISBN: 978-0-9837296-3-1

Additional resources at www.lancewoodbury.com

To my Grandparents
Roger and Grace Hamilton
whose life together exemplifies the
values in this book

Acknowledgements

THIS BOOK COULD NOT have been written without the insight and support of dozens of family enterprises I have consulted with over the last 15 years. My former partners at Kennedy and Coe, LLC, particularly Bill Jenkins and Kurt Siemers, saw the value of providing facilitation, mediation and family business consulting services, and encouraged and supported my development as practitioner. Three deceased family business owners were shining examples of the power of values: Barbara Perkins, Dan Snyder and Curt Watson. My major professor during college, Dr. Bill Long, has continued to serve as a mentor and was of tremendous assistance in organizing and editing this work. Finally, thanks to my wife Dana, whose patience, encouragement and care for me and our three children has made this book possible.

Introduction

IN MY ADOLESCENT years I lived with my family in Kansas City during the school year and my grandparents at the Woodbury Ranch in western Kansas in the summer. The farming and ranching operation, with some of the best irrigation water and native grass in the area, had been broken up to accommodate differences among the four siblings of my father's generation: my father had not returned to the farm, my aunt moved away, and the remaining two uncles farmed right next to each other on the family land but seldom spoke to each other. I witnessed first-hand the emotional pain of my grandparents as they struggled to understand why the family could not get along.

One summer, when I was 14, I approached my father and his three siblings to see if they would meet together to improve their relationship. To my amazement, they concurred. While I did not attend the meeting, I quickly made arrangements for their gathering. Though the family dynamics improved slightly after the meeting, the major impression left on me was the importance of initiating a family discussion, even if I didn't know exactly what I was doing at the time.

Little did I know that 25 years later I would be writing about a number of the values that have helped guide family businesses to better family interaction. After completing a graduate degree in conflict resolution, I was hired by the CEO of an accounting firm to help their clients work through the very same issues that my family experienced. Many of the firm's clients were farm and ranch families, so I knew something of their livelihood and I had experienced the conflicts most of them were trying to prevent.

After 15 years of consulting with hundreds of family and closely-held businesses (and managing a portion of the accounting practice), I decided to write about some of the beliefs and best practices that contribute to an enduring family business legacy. The process has reminded me that all family businesses have differences and disagreements, but that some are able to better manage those struggles and prevent more significant conflict. In fact, I often say that a dysfunctional family business is one in which everyone gets along! The key is not to avoid conflict, but to work together through the differences.

Why do some family businesses seem to successfully transition and grow when others fail? Even when families choose to split up the business, why are some are able to continue to interact positively? Why do some families in business, even if not the most financially successful, seem "wealthy" in terms of their fruitful interaction, their attitude of respect for one another and their long-term impact on their community and industry?

After pondering such questions, it became clear that one of the biggest contributors to a positive family business experience was the values exhibited by the family members involved in the operation. Those values (along with the money and the conflicts) have often been passed from one generation to the next, and they form a basis for family member interaction; they frame the canvas on which family business members paint their future. Such values might include regular communication, jointly defined goals, a desire to include spouses and in-laws, the use of capable advisors, and an ability to forgive one another, to name a few. Not every successful family business practices all the values in this publication, but most practice a good number of them.

The idea behind this practical book is not just

to describe to you the values witnessed in other organizations, but to encourage you to talk about your own family business values. You might choose one or two as a way to open a family meeting. Or read several and then try to identify the values that have shaped your family business. You could suggest your family business adopt a few of the values presented here. You might even give the book to another family business that might benefit from further reflection on their beliefs and practices.

However you choose to use the book, take some time to celebrate the many blessings you receive by participating in a family owned business!

Lance Woodbury
Garden City, Kansas
June 2012

One

The Value of Reflection

The Value of Reflection
(on Fundamental Questions)

IN A SPEECH TITLED "Solitude and Leadership" (published in the *American Scholar*, Spring 2010), William Deresiewicz discusses the importance of reflection in our lives—that process of "listening to yourself, to that quiet voice inside that tells you what you really care about, what you really believe in"—as a critical component of leadership. As I consider family business leadership, I echo Deresiewicz's thought: the process of individual family members deeply considering and reflecting on fundamental questions is absolutely critical to the effective functioning of a multi-generational or multi-sibling team.

A central issue that will guide me in these essays relates to the motivations, emotions, and beliefs in a family business in contrast to immediate goals or strategies for running the family business.

What often makes a family business better is the effective mix of individual perspectives coupled with the long-term commitment of family members. The ability of each family member to articulate his or her own unique and thoughtful viewpoint provides the building block for better analysis, and ultimately better decisions, by those managing the family enterprise. But articulating an original perspective comes only through first having reflected on why you believe what you believe. Individual reflection—having your own thoughts and knowing where you personally stand —becomes the foundation for family and business planning, and the discussions and shared knowledge that ultimately make the business better.

As you begin this book and reflect on your current situation, consider some of these fundamental questions: Are you happy in the family business? Why or why not? Why do you (do you?) want to be in partnership with family members? What are the financial, psychological and relational benefits of operating a business as a family, and what are the related costs? Then, as you feel comfortable answering these questions, you can move to more immediate ones: What should be the organization's priorities for the coming year? What obstacles need to be overcome? Finally, what are the outcomes, both personally and professionally, that would make the coming year the best year ever in your company and your family?

Answers to these questions, when thought through individually and then shared with your partners, can help build a better business, better relationships, and more clarity about the future.

Two

The Value of Honest Conversation

The Value of Honest Conversation

THE PREVIOUS CHAPTER considered the value of reflection: the importance of figuring out what you—as an individual—think and believe about your position or role in the family business, the direction and future of the company, and your relationship with your business partners and family members.

Just as important, however, is what you do with your reflections. While you might not share all of your reflections with your family business partners, it is important to have honest conversations so people know where you stand and so you can make decisions as an organization—decisions which almost always depend on the interests, goals and plans of key individuals in the company. Too many times the fear of conflict, the inability to communicate well, past grievances, or the hectic pace of the business cause much-needed conversations to go missed. Then the frustration builds, leading either to a blow-up or chilly disengagement. To have an honest conversation, you and the other person need to feel relatively safe, and this safety requires a degree of trust. (If you don't have these, should you be in business together?) Family business members must be able to feel that their dialogue can happen without compromising their personal safety, their confidentiality, or fearing that their comments will be used against them negatively.

Having an honest conversation also must go two-ways. You must, as Stephen Covey says, "seek first to understand, then to be understood." Even if you are the one that has to get something off your chest, you have to approach the honest conversation with the intent to listen to what the other person has to say. And that is really difficult. But the rewards can be grand!

In order to start an honest conversation, try the following:

1. *Make a list for yourself* of the subjects you would like to talk about, even writing a few sentences on each to capture your precise thoughts.

2. *Ask your partner* for a convenient and limited time, preferably no more than an hour, to talk about some important things for the company.

3. *Don't "dump" everything* at once. Try just one issue, with your feelings and your questions, in the first conversation.

On a scale of 1 to 10, how would you rate your ability as a family and/or business to have an honest conversation? Are there things that need to be said or discussed that you haven't taken the time to visit about?

Don't delay the honest conversation. The relief, clarity and certainty from such conversations can do wonders for family business progress.

Three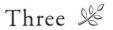

The Value of Listening

The Value of Listening

WHEN WRITING THE PREVIOUS chapter on the value of honest conversation, I mentioned how hard it is to really listen to others. LeRoy, a good friend of mine and a great listener, often reminds me that God gave us two ears and one mouth, and we should use them in such proportion. We should listen twice as much as we talk.

One reason that listening is so difficult in a family business is that, as family members, we are comfortable with one another. So comfortable, in fact, that we often don't afford family members the same degree of attention that we give non-family members, or even strangers! (In fact, as I write this on a flight to Chicago, my seat-mate Erin just complimented the flight attendant, who is now pouring out her life story and I think might actually cry any minute. What a good listener Erin is!) But just ask my wife, my brother or my sister how well I listen. By their reports you would never know I was trained in communication skills. Yet clients tell me they appreciate my listening skills. How can I be so good at communicating with some people, and so bad at communicating with others?

The reality is, we act as if we don't have to pay as close attention to those closest to us. We take for granted that they will always be there, that we can "deal with them later." So it goes with most family business partners. We interact with them on a frequent and historical basis, and too often we find ourselves formulating our response before they are finished, or we are thinking about more pressing issues, or we are even daydreaming, while a business partner or management team member—who also happens to be family—is talking directly to us. If we act like that with customers or non-family members, they quit interacting with us!

So how do you listen better? While there is no foolproof method to assure that you will really hear someone, the following steps provide the context for excellent listening.

1. *When you enter into a conversation, stop whatever else you are doing:* Turn away from the computer, put your pencil down, close the lid on the laptop. Show

the other person you are focusing on them.

2. *Use non-verbal communication*: Turn your body toward the speaker, make eye contact, nod your head in agreement that you understand.

3. *Ask questions that clarify the information or shed light on the details of what you are hearing.*

4. *Try to restate what they said*: "Jim, what I heard you say is..." Jim will tell you if you get it wrong. And if you get it right, Jim will feel that much better about you and your relationship.

The goal of listening should not just be to hear the words your partner says or even understand his or her your business position. Listening is ultimately about making your family business partner feel that his or her deepest sentiments have been registered, heard, internalized by you. Listening well is a gift you give to another, a gift that rewards both of you in the form of better business and family relationships.

Four

The Value of Vision

The Value of Vision

"WHERE THERE IS NO VISION, the people perish." This partial quotation from Proverbs 29:18 is sometimes mentioned in our business-centric world in reference to the importance of adopting a view of the future—"the vision" for a company or organization —that offers a rallying point for partners and staff pointing forward. But a closer read of this verse suggests that "vision" is really about having an understanding of God's purpose and learning how to align our purposes with God's. Note that the second half of the above verse is, "but happy are those who keep the law," which suggests that any vision we develop is based on something prior to the vision, something that needs to be nurtured or "kept." Vision keepers, therefore, are "law keepers," in the words of Proverbs or, alternatively said, are those who know how to root and keep their vision in practical realities of faith and wisdom.

As I work with family businesses to help them consider their future, I find myself drawn to this Biblical perspective of vision. What is the purpose of owning a business and working together as a family? Why do we put up with the conflicts between generations or siblings, the uncertainty of succession, or the frustration around the communication skills and behavior patterns of our partners? What is it that we are keeping?

Simon Sinek, in his book *Start with Why*, differentiates between what a company does (farming or ranching or dairying, for example), how they do it (using the values of land stewardship, being financially conservative, treating their landowners or employees well, etc.), and why they do it. In my conversations with agricultural family businesses, the "why"—what we're trying to keep—has to do with things like a love of the rural life, freedom, the chance to work with our kids, helping others, providing sustenance, building a community, or preserving a legacy for future generations. It just so happens that they are able to best practice this purpose—their "why"—in the field of agriculture.

The same holds true for those in other professions. For example, professional advisors (including your author) often believe deeply in helping others solve problems or in making a difference in others' lives. Accounting or law or wealth management or family business consulting just happens to be "what" they do to achieve their deeper purpose.

In my view, Sinek's "why" connects to Proverbs' "vision" and offers guidance for the future. Developing a sense of where you are headed—a true and relevant vision for the future—requires that you understand where you've come from. What has motivated you? What drives you today? How is that drive manifested in your business? What is it that causes your family members and staff to put their 100% in every day? Sinek suggests that when you can answer such questions— when you truly understand your "why"—the business and personal activities you might choose going forward greatly expand, thus offering guidance along your path to the future. At your next family business meeting, find out the "why" behind your partners' participation in the business. Discover what it is that your family business actually is "keeping." You might discover a key ingredient to a successful future!

Five

The Value of Progress

The Value of Progress

NOT LONG AGO, I led a planning session during which the organization I was working with laid out some fairly ambitious goals. After the workshop, I observed to the leader that quite a few of the outcomes, either because of unrealistic expectations or impossibility of measurement, would be difficult to achieve. For example, they set a goal of 25% revenue growth for the next year in the midst of a weak economy. Even if they had attained a respectable 10% increase, they might have felt like failures. Another goal was to require senior managers to develop "better supervision skills." But without any way to measure this goal, the words were almost useless.

Since that time, I've reflected much on the question of what constitutes measurable success or progress in a family business. As you look toward the future—or even evaluate your family business right now—how do you measure whether you are successful?

This conversation reminded me of a concept I learned about in the Strategic Coach program, a unique training and networking opportunity for entrepreneurs. Dan Sullivan, the founder of the program, in his short book *Learning How to Avoid the Gap*, gives his thoughts on what differentiates happy successful people from unhappy successful people. Both groups are successful, but one group seems pleased with their success, the other group seems dissatisfied. Why?

Dan suggests that the unhappy successful group measures its success relative to the ultimate vision. That ultimate vision, which he compares to the idea of the horizon (described as a mental model for thinking about distance, but something we never physically reach), has elements of our deepest aspirations, though it will probably never be fully achieved. Because people in this group focus on how short of the ultimate vision they have fallen, they often feel disappointment. They say to themselves, "We have not reached our destination. We can, and should, do more. We aren't getting the job done."

The happy group, on the other hand, looks back every now and then and recognizes how far it has come from the beginning. These people know that they may never fully achieve the ultimate vision, but they are able to see the vision as more of an alluring beacon rather than a set of fully achievable outcomes. Their happiness rests on their ability to look at how much they have gained since articulating their hopes, goals and dreams. They recall their starting point and celebrate the milestones along the way. They give thanks for their progress.

Thus, as you think of your success, do the following. Ask yourself:

1. What were some of the original milestones we established? and

2. How have they been fully or partially achieved? Then...

3. Recognize these milestones in the presence of your family business partners, in order to cultivate a mutual appreciation for your progress.

My hunch is that if you look back, you will gain immense satisfaction in recalling how far you've come. Having a vision is clearly important, and so is recognizing your progress along the way!

Six

The Value of "We" Knowledge

The Value of "We" Knowledge

A FARM FAMILY BUSINESS partner I know in Iowa includes this statement about his business efforts at the end of each of his emails: "Sustainably growing our business by transitioning 'I' knowledge into 'WE' knowledge." Those of us who consult with groups of people making decisions are well acquainted with this concept. The key to moving forward as a family business, or in any business, with multiple partners lies in those partners having a shared sense of something—the challenge, the opportunity, the solution, or the future. I call this shared sense of something "We knowledge."

I often refer to the process of getting to "We knowledge" as getting on the same page. Many problems in family businesses occur because partners do not have the same understanding of the challenge or goal or even of the situation in which the business finds itself. Each has his or her idea (the "I" knowledge) of what they are working toward, and each tends to frame all solutions based on how they individually see the problem. When the individual solutions conflict, the family business often encounters a stalemate.

Take, for example, how family members might think about the succession process. Typically the younger generation focuses on getting Mom and Dad to "let go," to turn over responsibility. In the same session, though, Mom and Dad want to see the kids "grab hold," to demonstrate their interest and capability in managing certain aspects of the business. Each of them frames the issue in a way implicitly critical of the other. While each generation's perspective is important, the shared challenge is really about managing a successful transition process for the benefit of both the business and family. It isn't about one or the other; it's about both perspectives. When reframed as the shared challenge, both generations need to adopt new practices.

If one redefines the potential stalemate into a shared definition or challenge, one can even identify new best practices—such as setting up an advisory board, joining a peer group, or obtaining additional education—as potential outcomes of developing "We" knowledge. That's the great thing about working to create a common view of the future. It can expand the range of possible solutions.

Here are a few tips for developing "We" knowledge.

1. Take the time to talk as a family business – by this you will begin to create the space for "We" knowledge and you will begin to see a common language to discuss problems and aspirations emerge.

2. Encourage everyone to participate.

3. Focus on arriving at a common definition of the challenge or goal, even down to the specific wording of the issue.

4. Commit to revisiting your progress on a regular basis.

You won't solve, and might not even fully define, the big issues in one meeting, so plan to keep working. Believe me, the long-term benefits of such planning —back to Matt's idea of business sustainability—far outweigh the short-term costs in time and efficiency.

Seven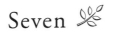

The Value of Outside Advisors

The Value of Outside Advisors

A COUPLE OF CLIENTS I work with often point out that if you think a good advisor is expensive, you should compare it to the cost of a bad advisor! So in honor of the annual tax deadline, quickly approaching as I write this essay, and recognizing that many family businesses use professional advisors (CPA's, attorneys, wealth managers, insurance agents, etc.), I thought I would offer some ideas on how outside advisors can be valuable to your family-owned business. At your next family business meeting ask these questions about your current team of professionals:

1. *Are they Competent?* Simply put, your advisors —your accountant, your lawyer, your insurance agent, your wealth management advisor and yes, even your family business consultant—should know what they are doing, and they should be doing it well. Who else

are they serving that face similar issues? How well are they doing at guiding you through the technical issues in accounting, law or wealth management? Are they respected by others in their field and by family businesses similar to yours? How well do they explain their analysis and advice?

Though your team may meet current needs, at some time in the future you may outgrow them. Or, alternatively said, you may need to align your advisors' ages more with your successors. Do you have the people you need with the knowledge and perspective to help you grow through the next stage of business development and family interaction? Or, is it time to consider other advisors?

2. *Are they Creative?* Your professional advisors should bring you ideas. The ideas need to be rooted in reality but the advisors should be thinking about your possible futures. Do they call with suggestions, giving you new ideas to consider or new ways to see the present situation? Or do they wait for your call and react to your questions? I remember a business owner who decided to diversify her investments. After a number of discussions initiated by her primary advisor, the strategy paid off by building significant wealth for her children. Are your advisors thinking ahead and helping you strategize?

3. *Do they Challenge you?* Do your professional advisors question you or do you do all the asking? Will your advisor take the risk of upsetting you? Do they say "yes" too much of the time? There is significant value – if your ego can handle it – in a team of advisors that supports you by, at times, pushing you. Chances are they have seen situations similar to yours and can help you considerably, if you give them permission, and they take the hint, to challenge you.

4. *Do they Collaborate with each other?* Will your professional advisors truly collaborate, or do you have to serve as the go-between, taking an answer from your accountant and running it by your attorney? In our increasingly specialized world, your advisor's ability to work well with other professionals, and sacrifice some ego for the benefit of the client, is critical to you receiving holistic advice. Occasional joint meetings and conference calls with several advisors at once should be part of your planning.

Many of you have advisors that do a great job on these points. At your next meeting, let them know how much they mean to your business and family! But if, for some reason, you aren't sure about your current team, ask the preceding questions and your own thinking will become clearer.

Eight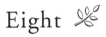

The Value of Inclusion

The Value of Inclusion

A PRIMARY SOURCE of family business conflict is to hold an important family or business discussion and not include some of the people who will be significantly affected by the decision. In a family business, there are lots of "outsiders" that we tend not to include—off-farm heirs, non-business spouses, the controversial sibling or spouse, or the life partner—and the results come back to haunt the family over and over again.

The following story, a composite of several experiences I have had, illustrates the issue. Dad, the founder of the family business, is finalizing his estate plan. Since the biggest part of his planning has to do with handing over the business, he calls a meeting of the three children who have been involved in the business, neglecting to inform the fourth child, who lives three states away and never has indicated an interest. The wife of this child catches wind of the planning meeting because she is in touch with the mother, who saw the planning meeting when she checked dad's schedule. This fourth child decides to hold a meeting with dad to talk about the estate plan, not including the other siblings. Very soon all the siblings become aware of the dual (and dueling) meetings and begin to suspect the others of ulterior motives. Chaos ensues.

This not-unusual scenario leads us to the simple question: does your family business communication and decision-making process contribute to, or detract from, family and business harmony?

My belief is that you should include, in some fashion, people who can throw a wrench in your plans. That "wrench" doesn't mean they can stop what you are planning to do; it means, however, they can sure make your life miserable while you are doing it. And the likelihood is that they will make your life miserable if the decision you make affects them or their immediate family.

Another family business consultant I know reminds his audience that your brother, sister, son or daughter working in the family business probably sees a "significant other" right before they go to bed and right after they wake up. And if that significant other doesn't like the communication and decision-making process in the family business, their dislike, mistrust, or frustration will most certainly spill over into your family and business relationships.

Inclusion does not mean that everyone in the family and all the spouses and significant others have to be involved in every meeting or decision. It does mean, however, that when considering important financial, estate or business structure decisions, you should think about ways to include a broader number of people.

As part of your planning for an important family business meeting, you should ask three questions:

1. Whose opinion should be *solicited* regarding things to discuss at the meeting?

2. Who should be *present* at the meeting and participate in the discussions?

3. Who should be *informed* of what happens at the meeting?

These questions assume that there is an interlocking hierarchy of expertise, experience and ownership that various members have, and this pattern of relationships needs to be analyzed and honored if the business is to go forward.

For example, prior to the meeting, you might conduct an on-line survey of family members to gather input. Or, you might have some less-involved family members participate in the research around a particular decision. Or, you might meet with smaller but more inclusive family units individually, then bring a representative of each family unit together for the strategic group discussion. The point is to be open to different methods to get people's thoughts on the table. Not only does doing so help prevent problems down the road, but it may give you new insights or ideas on the issue you are trying to solve.

However you decide to do it, I encourage you to err on the side of inclusion. It is sometimes more work in the short run, but can help the family business thrive in the long run!

Nine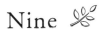

The Value of Waiting

The Value of Waiting

IN THE FAST-PACED and volatile business world of today, much emphasis is put on the ability to move rapidly and make quick decisions. We even have a vocabulary of quick action, including the ability to be "agile" or "proactive" or "forward-moving." Yet, business expansion opportunities, marketing decisions, and input cost minimization strategies often require a decision based on uncertain assumptions about the future or limited financial information. In the face of these realities, I'd like to put a plug in for the value of waiting—for slowing things down and taking some time on certain family business issues. Three dimensions of waiting readily come to mind.

1. *Waiting on what you say.* A while ago, through the good offices of a friend and client, I had the opportunity to attend the Berkshire Hathaway annual

meeting in Omaha. When Warren Buffet and his business partner, Charlie Munger, described their handling of a press release that dealt with unacceptable behavior of an employee, Charlie warned against saying too much out of anger. "If telling a man to go to hell is such a good idea, you can always tell him tomorrow." That's great advice in the family business. If you are angry, wait to discuss it until you've had a chance to cool off. The implications of speaking out of anger can last generations.

2. *Waiting on issues of partnership.* A number of families struggle with when to bring the next generation into the management of the business. Rather than rushing the process, even when people seem competent and committed, I often end up talking about the need to wait, to let them gain the experience and insight that can only be had working away from family members. Sending your child away and then waiting for your son or daughter to come back—when they want to come back and you want them to come back—is often nerve-wracking and painful. Perhaps, we think, the child will never come back. Perhaps she/he will find opportunities elsewhere. But over and over again I have seen problems arise from the lack of developing an outside perspective. On the other hand, we see the appreciation and knowledge and skill that young person brings back to the family business when

they have a chance to experience how other businesses work.

3. *Waiting on structural changes.* When making structural changes to the business, including adding new partners or splitting things up, it is important to give the issues some time to emerge and for everyone's thinking to evolve. One grower I know goes by this advice from his attorney: "figure out how to get OUT of business together before you get IN business together."

The point is that by creating a more deliberative process—by waiting—you usually arrive at better decisions. Issues of partnership or structural changes are usually very far-reaching, so waiting a few weeks or months while you are exploring will generally not hurt the organization. Note, however, that waiting does not mean avoiding the decision. It does mean that you should take some time to work through the options and develop your plans. Waiting, when used strategically, can do your organization much good.

Ten

The Value of Learning

The Value of Learning

MY GOAL IN ARTICULATING these values is to bring to light some of the best practices in successful family businesses. The hope is that you might learn something, either directly or through reflection, which will improve your organization. In this spirit I offer some comments about the learning process that I see going on in a number of growing and successful closely held companies.

A common theme among thriving family businesses is members' curiosity. Partners approach each event as a learning experience where there is something to be gained by better understanding a situation or the people involved. I sometimes watch these clients pencil out a competitor or vendor's business model, ask questions in an attempt to understand someone's motivations, test initial assumptions through dialogue with the person from whom they are learning, or read material that offers a contrary view to what they usually hear, all in hopes of better understanding others. They believe that increased comprehension offers new pathways to a better business.

(By the way, you might fit in this "curious" category if, every time you eat at a new restaurant, you find yourself watching customers, analyzing menu prices, and having conversations with the servers, all in a grand attempt to predict the restaurant's likelihood of success!)

As it applies to the family business, the learning I observe falls into a few categories:

1. *Learning more about your own business.* I watch successful businesses extract data from their financial systems, have discussions with one another and employees about what went well with various business activities (planting, harvesting, etc.), reflect annually on their accomplishments, and seek feedback from their customers or land owners in an attempt to better understand what is working—or not working—in their organization.

2. *Learning from other businesses.* I watch successful business owners interact with their peers in an attempt to glean knowledge or practices that might benefit their organization. Undergirding this desire to learn

from others is a level of humility, a willingness to say "we don't have it all figured out." They also see such learning as a two-way street—they are willing to share with others key insights from their successes and failures.

3. *Attending meetings and seminars.* I recognize that in most industries, and agriculture is no exception, there are more invitations to meetings than there are days in the year. I see successful family businesses strategically evaluating their seminar options, then choosing to participate in those conferences that offer a compelling benefit to their operation. And, the value often goes beyond the seminar topic to include the relationships that can grow through meeting other like-minded participants.

4. *Bringing it home.* A final learning component of successful family businesses relates to how people in the organization bring back their observations or lessons to share with their business partners. The best family businesses find a way to turn "I knowledge" gleaned from a relationship, discussion or meeting into "We knowledge" that benefits others in the business. They may write a report, present to others, or informally offer their significant take-aways, but the point is that they make sure their learning has a multiplier effect in the company.

As you consider how learning from others benefits your organization, I encourage you to hold your partners and your staff accountable to sharing their insights. I have no doubt your level of success will be enhanced.

Eleven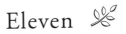

The Reconciliation Process

The Reconciliation Process

NEIL SEDAKA SANG to us that "Breaking up is hard to do" (in 1962, in case you were wondering). And while there is difficulty in breaking up a family business with all of the history and relationships and financial ties, reconciling with one another during or after a conflict in the family business is perhaps even harder. Continuing a relationship after trust has been broken or harsh words have been spoken takes a level of individual courage and resolve unlike most business interactions. Here is my view of what it takes to reconcile family business conflict—or any conflict with a person with whom you will have an ongoing relationship.

1. *Look to yourself.* To reconcile with another, I believe the best guidance and first step comes from the Bible. Matthew 7:4-5 asks "How can you say to your brother, 'Let me take the speck out of your eye,'

when all the time there is a plank in your own eye? You hypocrite, first take the plank out of your own eye, and then you will see clearly to remove the speck from your brother's eye." In other words, you first have to look at how your behavior or action has contributed to the conflict. Often the best way to see yourself is to ask a trusted colleague/friend/spouse to reflect back to you how she/he sees you in this situation.

2. *Empathize with the other.* Though we all have a sense of what empathy means—the ability to share the feelings of another—a brief journey into its origin will help us even more. Originally a 1909 English translation of the German word "Einfuehlung," empathy at first emerged in the aesthetic realm. It denoted the relationship of the artwork and the observer, who imaginatively projected him or herself into the object of contemplation. This idea of "placing oneself into" something else then became the root concept that was taken up in the developing field of psychology and bequeathed to us. It could refer to the ability to "place oneself into" another as he did a dangerous task (like a high wire act) or as she experienced grief or success. So successful has the term become in the last century that today there is a vigorous movement to understand the neurological basis of empathy, to discover the firing of

neural circuits that makes us able and eager to "place ourselves within" another.

Can you understand how the person with whom you are fighting feels? Can you see how they arrived at their point of view? That doesn't mean you agree with their actions, but you have to be able to step in their shoes and see it from their perspective. I often ask parties to articulate how the other person is feeling and why they might feel that way, in order to gauge the level of empathy.

3. *Be clear about what you need to move forward.* Restoring trust may require something from the family member with whom you are in conflict. What do you need to see or hear from the other person in order to begin restoring the relationship? An apology? Recompense of some sort? A commitment to, or refraining from, a certain type of behavior? From my perspective, a commitment to ongoing communication is absolutely critical to moving ahead. Communication offers a context for behavior, and provides a medium for clarifying assumptions and intentions.

4. *Recognize the role of forgiveness.* Forgiveness will be a value I'll write about in the future; for now consider this short reflection from Reinhold Niebuhr (sent to me by Rick Behrens):

"No virtuous act is quite as virtuous from the standpoint of our friend or foe as it is from our standpoint. Therefore, we must be saved by the final form of love, which is forgiveness." (Reinhold Niebuhr, *The Irony of American History*, 2008. p. 63).

Think about it as you read it again. We all consider our actions to be pure, but others never quite see it the same way. Our hope in continuing the family relationship is that our brother or sister forgives us for how we've hurt them.

Reconciliation is very tough work but without the commitment to doing it, family businesses often founder, staying mired in petty conflicts and backstabbing, ultimately breaking apart.

Twelve

The Value of Conflict

The Value of Conflict

THE LAST CHAPTER, on the value of reconciling, stressed the difficulty but essential nature of reconciliation in the family business. But in order to have reconciliation, you first have to have conflict, even though that same tension often can move your organization forward. Frequently, however, we think of conflict only in negative terms. But if managed appropriately, it can bring about healthy change.

Conflict, therefore, has a dual character, which is made clear by focusing on the little word "mine." I am not referring to the possessive pronoun "mine" but to the experience of earth exploration—mining. According to the *Oxford English Dictionary*, mining has the following meanings: (1) to dig in the earth, especially for treasure; and (2) to destroy by slow methods; to "undermine." If we "mine" something we are either seeking the most valuable treasure or we are ruining by slow or secret methods. This contradictory definition really makes sense, since any time you "dig," you might find treasure, or you might make the foundation, which stands above your digging, collapse.

Conflict is like that—it can lead to the discovery of real treasure or it can erode and destroy. Here are some ways to "mine" conflict for its value.

1. *Answer the following question: Is the conflict worth resolving?* While it may be uncomfortable to be in conflict, it may be manageable and sometimes can be beneficial to let it play out or not to intervene in it. How distracting or damaging is the conflict? Can you live with the tension or is it causing too much stress? If you can live with the awkwardness, then it may not be worth resolving. I say this because resolving conflict is also uncomfortable and takes hard work on the part of all parties. Resolving conflict requires you to be "all in" to make the situation better. Sometimes living with the conflict isn't as bad when you consider the alternatives!

2. *Recognize the benefits.* Conflict, and the willingness to engage in it, also has some benefits. If a party knows they will be confronted or held accountable for their actions (the "awkward" part of conflict), it may cause them to think twice about their strategy or current

path. It may encourage better communication because people know that not communicating will create some difficult future interaction. Conflict can also lead to the creation of new systems and processes to better manage the problems, and in family businesses, this can lead to increased professionalism. (Note, however, that if not managed, conflict can cause "professionalism" to go south in a hurry!)

3. *Understand the "why"—the interests of the other person.* When people are fighting, they often express a position—a "what". ("I want more money." "I want to control this part of the business." "I'm against your decision.") Conflict resolution encourages parties to ask "Why? What's behind your position?" For example, wanting more money can signal a need for recognition. A desire for more authority can relate to a person's sense of identity and their desired role in the organization. Being against certain decisions may actually represent a desire to be included earlier in the discussion, in order to provide more input.

To understand "why," try asking the person with whom you are experiencing conflict why their position is important to them. Ask them why they are upset. Ask them why they feel so strongly about their argument. If they choose to share the reasons behind their position, you have discovered some really valuable information that can help you shape solutions.

Careful attention to the dual possibilities arising out of conflict in a family business offers us the best opportunity for us to "mine" it for its value. Mining conflict carefully can enhance the family business. You can bank on it.

Thirteen

The Value of Exposure

The Value of Exposure

WHEN A LAWYER HEARS the word "exposure," he or she also hears the concept of liability and cringes. When doctors talk about "exposure," they speak about someone's physical vulnerability. But in business that term increasingly means what I mean here: a spirit of openness that looks outward for new possibilities of learning and service. Here are three ways you can broaden or extend your horizons.

1. *Exposure to uncomfortable situations.* This spring, a friend and client participated in a trip to one of the most uncomfortable places on earth now—Afghanistan. He went to understand what kinds of agricultural development might be needed as the country seeks to rebuild its infrastructure and the contribution our industry can make to such an endeavor. His trip provided not only a greater appreciation for the world

in which we live and a realization for how much we take for granted, but it also inspired him to improve his business because he has seen what a difference a good business can make to both a family and a society.

Other clients have participated in church mission trips and have returned with a renewed desire to improve the business, so that they might be in a position to continue directly helping others in less fortunate situations. The point is, by exposing yourself to radically different situations, you gain a renewed appreciation for your own assets, the inspiration to keep improving, and the desire to help others.

2. *Exposure to networks of like-minded business owners.* I facilitate a growing number of groups in which business owners come together to share information, learn, and challenge one another. This exposure offers a stream of new ideas, business philosophies and improvement strategies. Occasionally new business ventures or partnerships are born.

Other clients gain this exposure through industry leadership on boards and committees. The chance to spend a significant amount of time to develop relationships with others who have been successful in a different part of the country, or with a different agricultural business model, offers not just insight, but support. Family business members find such support extremely helpful when going through growth and change in their own business.

3. *Exposure to other types of businesses.* A number of clients and friends have chosen to invest in businesses other than production agriculture. Many initially invest to diversify financially, but they find that the exposure to a different business gives them a new lens with which to view their own organization. In short, they also gain diversity in perspective.

For example, seeing the human resource needs and structure in a bank offers ideas around managing employees at the farm. Seeing how a private equity fund thinks about their portfolio of businesses causes one to question one's own emotional attachment to a particular business model. Seeing how a massive wind energy project is organized can lead to new thinking around how major projects might be planned. Investing in a business further down the food chain brings reality to what really adds value to consumers. Investing in a tourist-town business causes one to think differently about customers and the service you might provide in your agricultural business.

As you consider your future, push yourself to broaden your horizons. The return may not always be financial, but the exposure will pay many kinds of dividends.

Fourteen

The Value of Vulnerability

The Value of Vulnerability

BUSINESS SUCCESS IS often the result of several factors: sound business strategy, financial acumen, wise capital decisions, hard work and discipline, good leadership...the list goes on and on. Family business success—particularly because of the family dynamic or system—includes another key ingredient: the willingness to be vulnerable to others.

What I mean by being vulnerable in a family business context is primarily the willingness of all family members to "own" their weaknesses; to admit they are not very good at some of the things that may be expected of them; to confess they may not have the answer; to be transparent. In short, one needs to be willing to ask for help.

In a safe and supportive environment, such vulnerability helps create powerful bonds among family members, who are really team members striving for the success of the business and for good relationships as family. Being vulnerable with one another builds the trust necessary to get through some of the growing pains your business will experience. But how do you become vulnerable to each other in a healthy way? Two ideas and two questions will clarify my thoughts.

1. *Owning your weaknesses.* Business and self-improvement literature is often geared toward getting better at something or removing your weaknesses. A different philosophy, to which I subscribe, suggests you should focus on your strengths and delegate your weaknesses. If you spend all your time working on weaknesses, you probably never really be strong at those things—you'll just be less weak!

To delegate your weaknesses, however, you first have to be honest about what they are. Too often, a family member openly admitting to others that they are not good at something is seen as too risky. They feel that the acknowledgement of a weakness might give ammunition to other family members, might influence the direction of the business or estate plan, or might damage their standing in a culture where strength—in everything—is expected.

2. *Creating a safe and supportive environment.* Admitting your weaknesses can only be done in

an environment where you feel that family members are committed to each other's success. If several siblings are vying for one leadership position, or are competing with one another for their parents' approval, then admitting a weakness will be difficult. If the business has several enterprises (cattle, crops, hay, a bank, etc.), with a family member responsible for each and judged solely on that unit's performance, the incentive to ask for help may be lacking. To sum up, admitting a weakness must be done in an environment where doing so is seen as necessary to move the business forward.

So, here are my two questions: (1) Do you have an organizational culture in which a family member (that means *you*) can safely admit weaknesses and ask for help? And (2) Are you willing to identify and discuss those vulnerabilities?

Madeline L'Engle writes "When we were children, we used to think that when we were grown-up we would no longer be vulnerable. But to grow up is to accept vulnerability...To be alive is to be vulnerable." (Madeline L'Engle, *Walking on Water: Reflections on Faith and Art,* p. 190). The aim in being vulnerable is to move past weaknesses, to strengthen trust and then to focus on each person's strengths. In my opinion, it's the fuel for family and business growth.

Fifteen

The Value of Certitude

The Value of Certitude

BENJAMIN FRANKLIN SAID that the only things certain in life are death and taxes. In family businesses—especially those in agriculture—there is often much uncertainty: the weather, the markets, your competitor's intentions, the regulatory and tax system, etc. Yet, I chose the word certitude, which connotes "a feeling of certainty", because in a family business, or in any working or family relationship, attaining confidence and certitude about the future is possible. And feeling more certain about the future is worth quite a bit when so many other things are unknown. Two stories will illustrate my point.

1. Many years ago a father asked me to facilitate several conversations between him and his two sons. In their adolescence, the brothers had experienced quite a rivalry. Recently, the second son had returned to the

business. As we talked about the future of the business, the now-adult sons did a nice job of discussing their goals for the business, their division of responsibilities, some of the areas that might cause conflict, and their plans to communicate with one another. The old rivalries were replaced by a common purpose.

At one point during the conversation, I looked over at Dad and saw he was weeping. At first, I thought this was a bit odd. From a facilitator's perspective the discussion was going quite well. I asked Dad if he wanted to share his thoughts, and he smiled through his tears and said he just wanted to be certain his boys would try to work together. Open dialogue brought certitude.

Several months later, Dad passed away. While unknown to me or other family members, Dad knew his time on earth was short, and he wanted some peace of mind around how his kids would handle the business and their relationship. Those facilitated conversations didn't guarantee family harmony, but they provided a feeling of certainty about where family members stood with respect to one another and their intentions to work together in the family business.

2. Fast-forward a couple of years to a different family, to a gathering where we were discussing the future of a family's retail business. From confidential interviews with family members, I knew that the kids

did not want to continue owning or operating the business. It wasn't their passion and the stress level was too high. With the parents aging and sensing a lack of enthusiasm in the kids, the whole situation seemed unsettled. Chances for family conflict were very high.

Through facilitated dialogue, the kids were able to tell their parents they really didn't want the business. Mom and Dad, much to everyone's surprise, were relieved to hear it! There was some disappointment that the business wouldn't continue in the family, but the parents had sensed the kids' lack of passion and were trying, through discussion, to arrive at some plans for the future. Once everyone knew everyone else's position, they developed a plan to sell the business. The family realized significant financial gain and the family relationship took on a healthier tone.

My point with these stories is that some of the better family businesses value the feeling of certainty that comes with hearing (not assuming) where their family members and business partners stand; with knowing their goals, concerns, intentions and plans.

How certain are you when it comes to other family members' thoughts and plans? I encourage you to have the dialogue—even if uncomfortable—that provides more clarity and confidence about the future.

Sixteen

The Value of Peer Interaction

The Value of Peer Interaction

AS A BUSINESS LEADER, with whom can you share your deepest business and family concerns? Who holds you accountable for business and family improvement? Who will be totally honest with you about the impact of your behavior? Who will challenge you to make the changes necessary for organizational growth?

Your spouse may not fully understand your business challenges. Your business partners may be too close. Other people in your business may tell you what they think you want to hear (or may even be afraid of you!). Your minister has great insight but hasn't run a business. Your paid advisors may hesitate to be brutally honest for fear of losing your business.

So, consider a peer group. Danny Klinefelter, leader of The Executive Program for Agricultural Producers (TEPAP) and its alumni organization AAPEX, has been encouraging the development of peer groups in agriculture. I recently spoke at his conference and suggested the following benefits to participating in a peer group.

1. *Community*. Owners of successful businesses in rural communities often feel lonely. Jealousy, envy or suspicion from neighbors, the competition for resources, or simply having a contrarian perspective can leave a successful owner feeling isolated. No one really understands your issues, will keep your concerns confidential, or will challenge you on the right issues. It can be an extremely difficult environment in which to sustain and enjoy your efforts to grow the business.

Joining a peer group, however, offers a chance to talk to others who share a similar perspective. A peer group supports and encourages your goals, plans, and ideas for improvement. Should you choose to accept it, a peer group offers some level of accountability for your actions. Honest conversation with a small group of peers—a community—can sustain your leadership effectiveness over time.

2. *Clarity*. The right group of business owners will challenge you to become clearer about your business strategy, often by comparing and contrasting with other participants. Your marketing methodology, compensation policies, land acquisition models,

employee management philosophy, and equipment strategies (just to name a few), all come under the microscope, forcing you to get clearer and clearer about why you do what you do.

The better you can articulate what you do and why you do it, the more likely other family members, key employees and business partners will be to execute the strategy. Clarity by you and others in your organization leads to increased focus and reduced confusion about how to be successful.

3. *Confidence.* While many differences exist between businesses, the right peer group will show some underlying, consistent patterns in how successful business owners think and act. How you treat in-laws or other family members, how you motivate and manage, how you think about investments, how you deal with landowners or tenants, or how you interact with your local community are a few examples of where you might see similarities. In turn you become more motivated and confident as your ideas, plans and goals are reinforced by others in similar situations. The correlation between your efforts and your success is confirmed by your peers. Your vision is indeed valid.

One of your jobs as a business leader is to create the right environment for improvement. The value that you and your family business can glean from participating in a small group that affirms, challenges and ultimately supports your growth should not be underestimated.

Seventeen

The Value of Forgiveness

The Value of Forgiveness

EARLIER I WROTE ABOUT the value of reconciling, suggesting that forgiveness played a large role in the ability to mend fences in the family business. Here are some additional thoughts on why forgiveness is such an important value—perhaps the most important but hardest to practice!

1. *Not if but when.* In every family business, there comes a time when someone either hurts you, or you hurt someone else. Often, but not always, such hurts are unintentional. I've seen the pain that comes from family members venting frustrations about one another too publicly, and the pain caused by venting only to a spouse; the pain caused by parents recognizing their kids' differences, and the pain caused by treating everyone equally; the pain created by not addressing tough issues, and the pain caused by one person

confronting another; the pain caused by blowing up, and the pain caused by staying silent. In any organization in which people work together, conflict is unavoidable. Your opportunity lies in how you deal with it.

2. *The Biblical imperative.* Faith plays a role in how I think about family business issues. In the case of forgiveness, there are many examples of our being called to forgive one another. One I like best is Ephesians 4:31-32:

"Make a clean break with all cutting, backbiting, profane talk. Be gentle with one another, sensitive. Forgive one another as quickly and thoroughly as God in Christ forgave you." (*The Message* translation).

Jesus was the embodiment of forgiveness, so if your faith is strong, how can forgiveness not be a value? It seems to me that the practicality here, if you are a person of faith, is that Christianity calls us—and helps us—to forgive at precisely the time when it is hardest for us to do so. Faith helps us do that which we cannot do alone.

3. *If you don't forgive, it will eat you up.* Louis B. Smedes wrote "To forgive is to set a prisoner free and discover the prisoner was you." I've watched family business partners or spouses hold on to anger, resentment and bitterness so deeply that they are

totally ineffective in moving the business forward. Their inability to forgive the other person creates missed opportunities to grow the organization and repair relationships. In several instances, that pent-up anger has ruined the next generation's interest or desire to continue the business. When so many issues are out of our control, what a shame to let anger be in the way our success.

Forgiveness changes everything. I once mediated between two owners, one of whom had conducted a business transaction behind the back of the partner in charge of that area. The conflict changed the nature of their relationship: trust was eroded, communication more guarded, their friendship lessened. Over time, however, forgiveness by the offended partner allowed their relationship in business to continue. Conflict had changed it from good to bad. Forgiveness, however, changed it from bad to better.

One final quote from Smedes illustrates my points: "Forgiving does not erase the bitter past. A healed memory is not a deleted memory. Instead, forgiving what we cannot forget creates a new way to remember. We change the memory of our past into a hope for our future." (Lewis Smedes, *The Art of Forgiving*, p. 171).

Eighteen

Valuing and Managing Transitions

Valuing and Managing Transitions

FAMILY BUSINESSES GO THROUGH a number of significant transitions. Transferring family wealth and business leadership, shifting to new management systems or governance structures, introducing new family members or non-family management, or selling and merging businesses all involve intentionally moving from point A to point B. How do successful family businesses navigate such transitions? Here are three examples of transitions and some of the best practices I see:

1. *Transitioning family assets.* When it comes to transferring assets, usually by way of an estate plan, successful families often first articulate their long-term goals. Minimizing taxes may be at the top of the list for some but, for others, contributing to a charity is important. Others may want to treat offspring equally,

while some want to reward those who returned to the business. Keeping a land base together might be critical, while others may want more flexibility and choice in how family members are invested together.

In order effectively to articulate their goals, family members often go through a period of reflection and then a process of gaining family member input. A team of good technical advisors can usually craft a plan that meets multiple goals, but they have to know your priorities. Successful families do a good job getting family members on the same page, outlining those goals and the level of importance ascribed to each one. Then they ask their professional advisors and advisory board members to hold them accountable for making progress.

2. *Transferring knowledge and skills* is another necessary family business transition. In order for the next generation to step up, they often need to get better at what the senior generation does, and gain perspective that comes through growth and development. Many will know the saying that "good judgment comes from experience, and experience comes from bad judgment." The chance to help your kids grow into a leadership role is a privilege some families never experience, as those who've lost their parents early can attest.

Giving the younger generation an opportunity to experience the consequences of their decisions and mistakes is crucial to effective management succession. Other tools that successful families use include development plans for each management team member (including honest feedback about where they need to improve), regular communication about their progress, ongoing education, a network of other multi-generational business-owning families, and often a stint working outside the family enterprise.

3. *Transitioning values.* As a mediator, I'm fond of saying that families often pass conflict and dysfunctional relationships from one generation to the next—right along with the assets. If brothers and sisters don't get along, the chances are pretty good that their kids won't have much of a relationship.

When you think about your family business, what are the values you want your current and future family business partners to exhibit? Stewardship, hard work, taking care of employees, industry leadership, philanthropy, humility, and faithfulness are a few positive values that I see. But I occasionally see greed, internal competition, avoidance, silence, secrecy, victimization, gossip, and poor employee treatment. Spend some time identifying and codifying those values that are most important to the legacy of your family and business. Write down specific examples of how those good values play out in your organization. And tell the stories that demonstrate those values throughout the history of the family business.

Transitions are inevitable and important. How you work through them says much about your organization.

Nineteen 🌿

Valuing Philanthropy, Giving Generously

Valuing Philanthropy, Giving Generously

PHILANTHROPY IS NOT A WORD frequently used among many families with whom I interact. Defined generally as "the disposition or active effort to promote the happiness and well-being of others," philanthropy, in the last few hundred years, has taken on the meaning of generous giving to good causes. While philanthropic action certainly benefits the recipients of gifts, my goal in this meditation is to encourage the practice of philanthropy or generous giving as a means of enhancing and developing the family business. Here are three benefits for family businesses that formally embrace philanthropy in their organizations.

1. *Holding the family together.* As businesses in general, and agricultural businesses in particular, see fewer children return to the company, giving money away or participating in activities to help those less

fortunate offers a chance for all family members to interact with one another. Participating in a charitable event or serving on a scholarship committee gives siblings and parents a chance develop and sustain relationships in a deeper way than just spending time socially as a family. It brings purpose and a level of discipline to their interaction, and it can reveal the diverse skill-sets among family members. Philanthropic activity can cultivate an appreciation for one another in a way that social activity, or even business activity, cannot. In more than one instance, I have seen how philanthropic activity in a family business gives new direction to individual family member's lives, igniting a passion for service and understanding that previously was absent.

2. *Broadening the family legacy.* Every community has business-owning families who are recognized for their success. But I know a few family businesses whose legacy is more than business success: their legacy is about the difference they make in the lives of others. It seems to me, at least anecdotally, that those difference-making organizations generate more enthusiasm and better morale among employees. They are talked of more positively in the community. They are sought out frequently for partnership opportunities, and they often contribute positively to the image of their industry. Their charitable activity doesn't necessarily

make them more or less profitable, and they often don't seek the spotlight. However, when you look back over 50 or 100 years, it is those philanthropic families who are seen as having made the world a better place.

Mike Miller, a friend who works for Mennonite Economic Development Associates, has many stories about businesses whose success in North America has been strengthened through their participation in activities to alleviate poverty in developing countries. It really works!

3. *Communicating important family values.* The decision to involve family members in charitable acts—the giving of money, resources, time or talents in the service of others—provides a powerful medium for communicating what the family truly values. As a trustee of the Finnup Foundation of Garden City, Kansas, I constantly have the founders' value in mind as I make grants or interview prospective grantees. When I talk with agricultural families, I often hear them talk about how they want to perpetuate the values that have made them successful. For example, some value their management of land, which enters into their gifting of financial resources as they become more successful. I know several family business owners who value a college education and thus fund scholarships for employees or community members or give directly to schools for this purpose. I've seen family business

members who value helping those in extreme poverty and so they encourage mission trips or participation in Habitat for Humanity projects. The point is that philanthropy or generous giving can shape future generations by identifying and communicating the core principles of family business members.

Doing philanthropy well—giving money away to effect change, or using your time and energy productively to serve others—is not an easy task. The dividend, however, can be much greater than any financial reward. Good family relationships, a positive influence on future generations, and an enduring legacy are assets that truly are a family business's wealth.

Twenty

The Value of Tackling Tough Issues

The Value of Tackling Tough Issues

AT VARIOUS POINTS in the history of every family business, really tough decisions loom. It could be the decision by a family member to leave the business or call an end to the current business partnership. It might involve closing a division or voluntarily giving up some farmland to restructure the business. It may mean saying "no" to your son or daughter who wants to return but really isn't ready—and taking the risk that they may never return to the company or, worse, to home. It may be a decision to treat children unequally in an estate plan. For parents, siblings and children in business together, such decisions are at best uncomfortable and at worst can invoke serious anxiety, and can be relationship-altering events.

Some tough decisions may be preventable with good communication and family business policies. But there will always be difficult decisions you can't foresee. There are simply too many situations, too many personalities, too many inherent conflicts between family behaviors and business requirements, and too many factors outside of your control to coast through the life cycle of a family business without some conflict or pain around certain choices. In this chapter I will mention three things to *avoid* and then three things to *do* when important decisions impend.

Three Things that Unsuccessful Family Businesses Do

1. *They simply avoid or deny the importance of a major issue.* They continue as if the issue will magically resolve itself or fade away. Perhaps they think they can wait it out. Unfortunately, it seldom works that way and in the meantime, morale, motivation, relationships and business performance all take a hit.

Take, for example, an unresolved conflict between father and son. The tension in the relationship makes it difficult for people to be around them when they are together, yet family business success in today's environment often calls for collaboration, communication and joint-problem solving. Their inability to work out their differences means the business is not operating at an optimal level.

2. *If they don't avoid the decision or issue, they go around in circles when they try to resolve it.* Every meeting ends in a heated exchange. Family members know one another's "triggers" and every attempt to find the answer results in an argument.

3. *An even worse, but all too frequent, scenario is when family members decide they can't do anything about the tough issues, so they become resigned to "taking care of Number One."* They give up on trying to work collaboratively. Decisions become more unilateral. People stop sharing information. The individual becomes focused on their financial success and not on the family or organization's success. When people resign, yet continue working for the business, it is the beginning of the end.

Three Things that Successful Family Businesses Do

1. *They don't hide from the decision.* Successful family businesses don't walk away from the discussion. They get the issue on the table—however difficult—in order to move beyond it. And they keep working on it so that there is progress, even if it results in a different structure or a smaller business or a period of very awkward interaction. They hold to the idea that "all progress begins by telling the truth," and the truth is that they have a difficult issue to work through! As

you commit to holding each other accountable to the truth, you may find it necessary to get an outsider involved to force and guide the conversation.

2. *They remind each other of the consequences of not resolving the issue.* Whether it is poor business performance, future legal disputes, or sour family relationships, the cost of inaction on difficult issues can be a significant motivator. Similarly, remind yourself of the benefits of reaching agreement in order to pull you through difficulty.

3. *They work harder to understand family member's motivations.* Seeking to understand why people feel the way they do through good questions, and recognizing their behavioral styles and motivating factors will help in creating options and working together more effectively. With respect to this last point, I have found instruments such as the DISC psychological inventory or Kolbe assessments helpful to use.

However you do it, I encourage you to make tackling tough issues a family business value. The willingness to deal with the tough decisions now will set the stage for future family business success.

Twenty One

The Value of Thankfulness

The Value of Thankfulness

THOUGH ESPECIALLY CELEBRATED AT end-of-the-year occasions, thankfulness really is always in season. This was brought home to me recently when I attended the Mennonite Economic Development Associates Conference in Lancaster, Pennsylvania. While I spent most of the weekend trying to pronounce "Lancaster" correctly (it is LANK us tur, rather than what I, on the analogy of KAN SAS (i.e., LAN CAS ter), wanted to make it), I learned a great deal about gratitude while there. I heard entrepreneur after entrepreneur in the private sector, almost all of whom represent closely held businesses, speak about the way he or she was using the fruits of success to impact the poor in developing countries. Though most of them showed a forward-looking blend of humility, generosity and impact, the most impressive characteristic that came across was thankfulness.

It made me reflect on what were some of the constituent elements of gratitude, and what family businesses could do to cultivate an attitude of thankfulness in their work. Three things came to mind.

1. *Recalling success.* One family business I know catalogs their personal and business accomplishments for the year and discusses those annually as a group. Not only does the exercise remind them of how much progress they've made (it sometimes doesn't feel that way when the alligators are nipping at the seat of your pants), the activity also causes them to express gratitude to the others who make the business work well.

At a number of other family business gatherings I've facilitated over the years, meetings have started with each person reflecting on something for which he or she is thankful. Starting a family discussion or any business meeting this way sets a cooperative and productive tone for further discussion. One other technique is to recall, as a family, how generations past have persisted through hardship to create the opportunities that family members now enjoy. Thus, a good part of thankfulness is cultivating and celebrating our common memories as family and business associates.

2. *Contrasting experiences.* Several family businesses I'm acquainted with spend time far away—literally and figuratively—in the places opposite to what we might consider "successful": poor villages, international zones of crisis, natural disaster sites, orphanages and hospitals, soup kitchens and homeless shelters. The stark contrast to the material riches and opportunities we enjoy in our business and personal lives cause participants to pause and reflect on how much we take for granted. For those who have ears to hear and eyes to see, experiences of this sort also impart levels of knowledge and perspective not gained by simply staying home. The stories of hardship or abuse, the examples of endurance and the happiness and sparks of hope they witness among those less fortunate make our complaints seem quite trivial. The experience reminds us we have much to be thankful for.

3. *Sharing faith.* One other source of a thankful perspective is the shared belief in something bigger than the business or family. I've watched thankfulness emerge from family members by beginning meetings with devotions or prayer, wrapping up a tough discussion in order to go to mass together, or giving a percentage of profit to churches, charities or other faith-based organizations. The idea that their efforts in business are for a greater cause, that they are blessed, that they are stewards and trustees of a good heritage,

and that God "expects much;" all these things serve as a call to appreciate the blessings they have received.

A verse that always comes to mind when the subject of thanksgiving emerges is Colossians 3:15: "Let the peace of Christ rule in your hearts, since as members of one body you were called to peace. And be thankful."

Twenty Two 🌿

The Value of Wealth

The Value of Wealth

IN A BUSINESS or financial setting, "wealth" often refers to the numerical values on a balance sheet or personal financial statement. I've long believed that "true" wealth is much broader and is indicated by good family relationships, a positive influence on future generations, and an enduring legacy. And while there is no traditional place to list them on the financial statement, here are a few more off-balance-sheet indicators of family business wealth.

1. *Commitment.* In some family enterprises, I hear partners say "family relationships take priority over the business." What they usually mean is that if the business relationship creates too much tension or stress in the family, they will find a way to stop working together. While this approach, valuing people over business, appears virtuous on the surface, it usually is

fraught with unspoken problems. First, by the time tension has prompted a business exit, the damage done to the family relationship is significant and often irreparable. (Family and business are not so cleanly separated.) Second, this approach implies that healthy relationships are defined by the absence of tension or conflict, instead of by the ability to work through such differences.

A more realistic approach is to admit that at times throughout your working relationship there will be tension—sometimes severe—and that the importance of the relationship requires more time spent working through those differences. In other words, your commitment to resolve conflict as family members and business partners is a better indicator of wealth than the absence of conflict in your organization or dissolving the business when problems arise. Simply put: wealthy family businesses commit to work through their differences.

2. *Presence.* With ongoing business demands, the day-to-day needs of customers, suppliers, and employees, email, text messages, cell phones, news media, market updates and social networking, it is increasingly difficult for business partners to be fully present with one another. Our attention to a busy world creates an environment where communication

is truncated and important thoughts and concepts are not fully expressed. This lack of presence slowly chips away at the foundation of good relationships.

In contrast, think about the good conversations you've had when not distracted, when you've invested in being present. A long drive or airplane ride together, an early morning meeting or cup of coffee with someone, or even a focused discussion after a negative incident, all tend to elicit the response: "we should talk about these things more often!" Indeed, one of the most important gifts you can give to another is to be fully present, focused on that person so they feel valued and you develop the ability to listen well. Wealthy family businesses find ways to create opportunities for members to be present with one another.

3. *Contribution.* At both a business and a personal level, people want to know they are making a meaningful contribution. People in agriculture businesses feed the world. Professional advisors help clients. Those in philanthropy and not-for-profit enterprises improve the lives of those struggling or who are less fortunate. Managers in businesses develop staff. Employees create a positive team environment. I once met the training director for a well-known five-star hotel and she talked about guest service as a "ministry" to others (she in fact had a Master of Divinity degree). In wealthy family

businesses, owners and staff have a sense that they are at some level making a contribution to the organization, its customers, or one another.

Finally, and this point could fit in a number of these meditations, an indicator of true and lasting wealth will be the shared experiences we recall and hold dear. Wealthy family businesses capture the stories and cherish the memories they create together. As you think about your business, I encourage you to consider a broader definition of wealth, a definition that accounts for the many non-financial assets that comprise your "true" balance sheet

Twenty Three

The Value of Ownership

The Value of Ownership

MUCH LIKE THE DISCUSSION about wealth in the previous chapter, the word "ownership" typically brings to mind certain financial concepts: possessing assets like land or equipment, controlling shares of stock or units in a LLC, achieving a target return on investment or a certain return on equity, receiving distributions or dividends. This chapter, however, focuses on a different kind of ownership in your family business—what I call *psychological* ownership.

By psychological ownership I mean a sense of dedication, a feeling of investment, a demonstration of commitment by your family members, business partners and key employees that cannot be gained solely through financial means. It's the feeling of ownership that comes with their belief in the organization and the team of people working together to succeed. This sense of ownership proves so elusive to larger companies, but I witness it over and over again in many family businesses.

Over the years of observing closely held enterprises, I see at least five ingredients that contribute to psychological ownership:

1. *Vision as a family in business together.* Here the emphasis is on "family." Beyond having a sense of direction and being excited about where the business is headed, members desire to interact in the future not simply as a business but especially as a family. Many actually emphasize the value and time spent working on the family relationship. This might include "checking in" with one another during difficult times, spending time having fun as a group, saying thanks to a family member, dedicating some non-business time together, or including young kids in some of the business activities.

2. *Role.* Psychological ownership increases when people understand their unique role in the family business. In contrast, conflict and disengagement often occur when there are not clear understandings about family members roles in relation to one another, or a clear path to making a valued contribution in the family's or enterprise's pursuits.

3. *Control.* One of the key ingredients in family business succession—which you might consider the

ultimate result of psychological ownership—is the ability to make relevant decisions and to suffer the consequences of the wrong ones! If the incoming generation doesn't get a chance to call certain shots, you run the risk of losing their potential ownership interest. The reality is that even if the incoming generation makes a mistake or a poor decision, it won't be so big that you can't fix it. Give them a chance.

4. *Legacy*. Another important ingredient in psychological ownership is a sense that members are creating an opportunity for future generations. The idea that you are building something that will be a blessing to others is a powerful reason to engage. The legacy may or may not be the business as it stands today, but may include what the business provides, whether a land base, a future income stream, philanthropic opportunity, business start-up capital, a house, educational resources, or even a way to teach certain values to future generations.

5. *Success—broadly defined*. A final key to psychological ownership is the ability for members to realize their own definition of success through the family business. For some, success will be defined financially, but for others it might be the number of jobs they provide as a business, or the flexible time they can use to spend with their family, or the contribution they make to the local, national or global community.

True ownership occurs when people see the family business as contributing to their own idea of a life well-lived.

Psychological ownership is the foundation of long-term business achievement. So consider how engaged each of your family members and business partners are in your family and business endeavors. You might even "score" your accomplishments on the five factors listed here as a way to jumpstart the conversation!

Twenty Four

The Value of Service

The Value of Service

AS WE NEAR THE END of our reflections on family business values, we come to one value that not only permeates several others but that exists in some of the most respected organizations with which I am acquainted. That value is service. And I don't mean service as in the act of "customer service," as when an economic transaction occurs between parties and they treat each other politely. I am instead referring to the attitude of service some business owners and family members exhibit, a stance in which they continually seek to meet the needs of other people in significant ways. Let me offer a few examples of how this value of service is manifested:

- A sister in the business cares for her non-business sibling by attending to her personal affairs, with no expectation of recognition or remuneration.

- A father honors his children and their growth in the business by beginning to step away from it at a point which others might view as the prime of his career. (The next generation will not realize for another 20 to 30 years how hard it is to step away at the point their father is choosing to do so.)
- A daughter supports her father by carrying significant family business burdens, without the father's knowledge, during a time when Dad's medical and emotional problems are significant.
- A CEO considers his employees' welfare by including their spouses and family members in social and educational activities and trips, thus giving them a chance to strengthen their relationships.
- Business owners serve their community through anonymous contributions to organizations that have no bearing on their business interests—and no PR value for the company.

The Swiss theologian Karl Barth defined service as

> ...a willing, working and doing in which a person acts not according to his own purposes or plans but with a view to the purpose of another person and according to the need, disposition and direction of others. It is an act whose freedom is

limited and determined by the other's freedom, an act whose glory becomes increasingly greater to the extent that the doer is not concerned about his own glory but about the glory of the other. (Karl Barth, *Evangelical Theology: An Introduction*, 1963. p. 184).

The family businesses that operate in line with this definition of service radiate contentment and peace unlike others I know. A compelling notion of service is also described in Robert Greenleaf's work on "servant leadership," in which he articulates the idea that the "great leader is seen as servant first, and that simple fact is the key to his greatness."

The business owners of whom I'm thinking appear to operate with a primary motivation toward the growth of others. In fact, one of Greenleaf's criteria for servant leadership is whether those served "become healthier, wiser, freer, more autonomous, more likely themselves to become servants."

Finally, as we think of the central message of Christianity, recall Eugene Peterson's translation of John 13:13-17:

You address me as 'Teacher' and 'Master,' and rightly so. That is what I am. So if I, the Master and Teacher, washed your feet, you must now wash each other's feet. I've laid down a pattern for you. What I've done, you do. I'm only pointing out the obvious. A servant is not ranked above his master; an employee doesn't give orders to the employer. If you understand what I'm telling you, act like it - and live a blessed life. (*The Message* translation).

Family business members who demonstrate the value of service live a blessed life indeed.

Twenty Five

The Value of Values

The Value of Values

WHEN I BEGAN WRITING these essays, my leading idea was to encourage readers to consider the guiding principles that shape their family business experience. Emphasis is often placed on the financial legacy of a family enterprise, while the beliefs and behaviors— the culture that created success—are not adequately articulated. As I finish these essays, I am even more convinced of the centrality of focusing on values in family business.

As I was writing this final essay, I heard Bill Cordasco, the President of Babbit Ranches in Arizona, describe their family's Constitution, which is a document outlining their values as an organization. He talked about how articulating those values had guided the organization through key decisions and had helped to frame how they approach problems, new opportunities and even their interaction with the local community.

While you may not give your values document such a grand title, here are two ways your family business can benefit by articulating your values in writing:

1. *Clarify expectations and guide decisions.* As commitment to the original vision may wane over the course of time, the values you express in writing codify your standards, providing a point of reference as to how you expect others to behave. Printed in black and white, you can directly link the reasons for a decision to a key doctrine in the family or business. These linkages, when expressed over and over again, call forth an expectation that the key principles of the past will play a central role in your future.

Personally speaking, I can trace my own commitment to "improvement," whether assisting a family business, a professional services firm, or a rural community, directly to my father and to his father and even to his father. They all believed in leaving something better than they found it. I know this ethic is not particular to me or to my family, but if I use the value as a guide to my future decisions, it helps to focus my energy toward the places and organizations on which I can make the biggest difference.

2. *Give everyone a chance to participate in the discussion.* Many family businesses face the issue of not

having everyone return to the enterprise, or having in-laws or spouses that don't spend time in the business. Real frustrations can develop when the conversation at Christmas or Sunday dinner continues to turn to day-to-day business issues, yet not everyone around the table can participate in the discussion due to their knowledge level or lack of experience.

Focusing the conversation on values, however, gives everyone a chance to participate, because values have broad application. The value of learning, for example, can be seen not only in seminars for family business managers, but in the education and experience of all family members. The value of forgiveness applies to any relationship. The value of service can be expressed in any endeavor in which one does something for another—an economic transaction, a marriage, or an act of neighborliness. The expression of the value is not limited to what happens in the business, and as such invites others to share their experience.

My hope for you is that you will identify your family business values and then create time with your family and business members to talk about how those values are lived daily. The family enterprise that identifies its core principles creates a legacy that far outlasts its financial or material success. Identifying and articulating values builds the character of future generations.

Made in the USA
Lexington, KY
12 December 2012